achomlishments (accomplishments) Alcaida [illegible]d
(allowed) Amendmen (Amendment) apologizes (apologies) are
(our) attaker (attacker) Barrack (Barack) Bengahzi (Benghazi)
Bidan (Biden) Boarder Security (border) capital (capitol)
chanded (changed) cheif (chief) chocked (choked) chocker (choker)
covfefe (coverage) Columbia (Colombia) colusion (collusion)
Marine Core (Corps) councel (counsel) council (counsel)
dieing (dying) discgrace (disgrace) discribing (describing)
W.E.B. DeBois (DuBois) do (due) dummer (dumber) eminent
(imminent) Esperanto (Esper) Generel (General) hamberders
(hamburgers) hear by (hereby) hearby (hereby) heel (heal)
highjacked (hijacked) honer (honor) honerd (honored)
honered (honored) Hose Republicans (House) inocent
(innocent) its (it's) it's (its) Kim Jung Un (Kim Jong Un) Bobby Night
(Knight) leightweight (lightweight) liable (libel) loose (lose) text
massages (messages) Melanie (Melania) missle (missile) moot
(moat) Deven Nunez (Devin Nunes) outrages (outrageous) payed
(paid) peach (peace) principal (principle) prople (people) pour (pore)
privet (private) reaspected (respected) roll (role) Rupublicans
(Republicans) San Bernadino (San Bernardino) Secretary of Educat-
uon (Education) seperation (separation) Sepulcher (Sepulchre)
shoild (should) shoker (shocker) Smocking Gun (smoking)
Somolia (Somalia) tapp (tap) tarrifs (tariffs) Teresa May
(Theresa) to (too) unpresidented (unprecedented) waist
(waste) waite (wait) wether (whether) wonerful (wonderful)
Chinese President Xi Xinping (Jinping) Zellinsky (Zelensky)

LEWSER!

Recent Collections

Virtual Doonesbury
Planet Doonesbury
Buck Wild Doonesbury
Duke 2000: Whatever It Takes
The Revolt of the English Majors
Peace Out, Dawg!
Got War?
Talk to the Hand
Heckuva Job, Bushie!
Welcome to the Nerd Farm!
Tee Time in Berzerkistan
Red Rascal's War
Squared Away
The Weed Whisperer
Yuge!: 30 Years of Doonesbury on Trump
#SAD!: Doonesbury in the Time of Trump

Anthologies

The Doonesbury Chronicles
Doonesbury's Greatest Hits
The People's Doonesbury
Doonesbury Dossier: The Reagan Years
Doonesbury Deluxe: Selected Glances Askance
Recycled Doonesbury: Second Thoughts on a Gilded Age
The Portable Doonesbury
The Bundled Doonesbury
40: A Doonesbury Retrospective

Special Collections

Flashbacks: Twenty-Five Years of Doonesbury
Action Figure!: The Life and Times of Doonesbury's Uncle Duke
Dude: The Big Book of Zonker
The Sandbox: Dispatches from Troops in Iraq and Afghanistan
The War in Quotes
"My Shorts R Bunching. Thoughts?": The Tweets of Roland Hedley

Wounded Warrior Series

The Long Road Home: One Step at a Time
The War Within: One More Step at a Time
Signature Wound: Rocking TBI
Mel's Story: Surviving Military Sexual Assault

LEWSER!

More Doonesbury in the Time of Trump

A DOONESBURY BOOK
by G. B. TRUDEAU

Andrews McMeel
PUBLISHING®

DOONESBURY is distributed internationally by Andrews McMeel Syndication.

Andrews McMeel Publishing
a division of Andrews McMeel Universal
1130 Walnut Street, Kansas City, Missouri 64106

www.andrewsmcmeel.com

20 21 22 23 24 RR2 10 9 8 7 6 5 4 3 2 1

ISBN: 978-1-5248-5950-3

Library of Congress Control Number: 2020930893

DOONESBURY may be viewed on the Internet at
www.doonesbury.com and www.GoComics.com.

PREFACE

"I take no responsibility at all." — Donald Trump

When POTUS was asked at a press conference whether he took any responsibility for the slow response to the pandemic, I sent a silent prayer heavenward: Please let him say more than just "no." Prayer answered! Not only did Trump serve up a direct denial, he added a cherry ("at all"), creating the perfect meme for his enemies, one that will be tattooed across his forehead throughout the fall campaign. Tens of thousands of deaths, and none of them due to his incompetence? Not even the couple that drank fish tank cleaner? Nope, not his fault.

Did Trump understand what he'd said? Likely yes, and by the time you read this, he will have doubled and tripled down. Whenever his support is on the verge of expanding—which often happens to a president during a crisis—he undercuts the momentum with some new deeply abrasive affront. Forty-six percent plus voter suppression, he believes, is a winning formula. It worked once, it will work again.

For a citizenry worn down by years of such outrages, and demoralized by a seeming eternity of self-storage, what's left but to laugh? As Twain once wrote, "The secret source of humor itself is not joy but sorrow." So on Twitter, a video recently went viral. A middle-aged man is being interviewed. "You have a choice," he is told. "Do you (a) quarantine with your wife and child, or (b) . . ."

"B!" shouts the man.

Even in pitch dark, comedy always finds its way. It is sometimes mistakenly assumed that hyperbole is satire's sharpest tool and that a presidency of such extremes as this one is surely beyond its reach. But there are a million ways to hold up the mirror. When Beyoncé announced she was pregnant with twins, a wit from Ireland tweeted, "Sad that there are more black people in Beyoncé right now than in Trump's entire cabinet team."

And then there was this: Trump tweeted, "The United States cannot have a better, or smarter, person representing our country than Ivanka." To which someone replied: "Why not?"

Hey, Someone. We who crack wise for a living salute you. Stay safe.

Garry Trudeau
April 10, 2020

"Just remember, what you're seeing and what you're reading is not what's happening."

— President Donald J. Trump

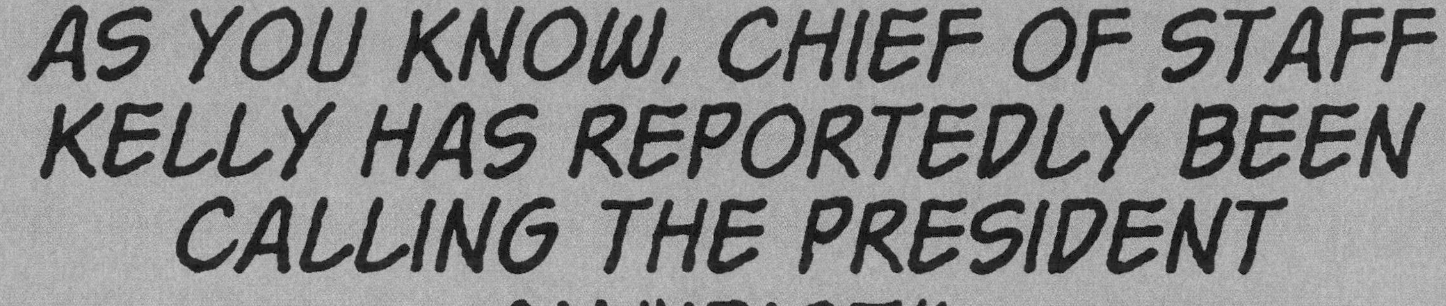
AS YOU KNOW, CHIEF OF STAFF KELLY HAS REPORTEDLY BEEN CALLING THE PRESIDENT AN "IDIOT"...

PART 1
The Stable Genius

SARAH, IF YOU COULD JUST CLEAR UP ONE THING FOR ME...
WHAT'S THAT, ROLAND?

AS YOU KNOW, CHIEF OF STAFF KELLY HAS REPORTEDLY BEEN CALLING THE PRESIDENT AN "IDIOT"...

... JOINING REINCE PRIEBUS AND STEVEN MNUCHIN, WHO ALSO CALLED HIM AN "IDIOT."

BUT REX TILLERSON CALLED HIM A "MORON," H.R. MCMASTER CALLED HIM A "DOPE," AND GARY COHN SAID HE WAS "DUMB AS S---."

SO WHICH ONE IS IT? WE'VE BEEN GETTING **VERY** MIXED MESSAGES!

WOW, ROLAND!
SUCH A GOOD QUES-TION!
WHAT? REALLY?
LOOK, THE PRESIDENT IS A STABLE GENIUS. HE'S BEEN VERY CLEAR ON THAT.
GBTrudeau

June 3, 2018

SO ACT NOW AND PICK AN ACTION ITEM **TODAY**!

MAIL TO:
KEEP AMERICA GREAT!
TRUMP TOWER
NEW YORK, NY 10021

Dear Trump 2020:
Please use my donation of $_____ to:
☐ stop Mueller ☐ stop impeachment
☐ stop Stormy ☐ enrich Trump
☐ enrich campaign manager ☐ misc.

NAME
ADDRESS
CITY STATE ZIP

GBTrudeau

May 20, 2018

HOW RIDICU-
LOUS IS THIS?
SORRY?

THIS PLAYGROUND! IT'S **SO** SAFE AND STERILE! EVERYTHING'S RUBBERIZED AND LOW TO THE GROUND!

KIDS HAVE A BASIC NEED TO EXPERIENCE RISK, TO FACE FEAR AND OVERCOME IT. THAT'S HOW THEY BECOME CONFIDENT.

BUT THIS PLACE? MY GUYS ARE TOTALLY BORED HERE!
WHICH ONES ARE YOURS?

THEY'RE RIGHT OVER THERE.
UM... OVER WHERE?

ACROSS THE STREET– IN THE DUMPSTER.
BOYS! WAVE!
OKAY, SO I'M CALLING THE POLICE.

May 29, 2016

WE'RE BACK FOR ANOTHER EDITION OF OUR SERIES "TEACH YOUR CHILDREN WELL"...

... AND MY GUEST IS OKLAHOMA PUPIL-ACTIVIST EMMA McNEIL. WELCOME, EMMA!
THANKS.

SO I UNDERSTAND YOU AND YOUR FRIENDS JOINED YOUR TEACHERS DURING THEIR RECENT WALKOUT. HOW COME?
WE ALL LOVE OUR TEECHERS...

... AND WE SUPPORT THEIR DUMANDS FOR FAIR PAY AND ADAQUIT FUNDING FOR OUR SCHOOLS, WITCH ARE A DISGRACE.

OUR TEXBOOKS ARE CRUMBLING, OUR CLASSROOMS LEEK, AND A **FIFTH** OF HOUR SCHOOLS ONLY MEET FOUR DAYZ A WEEK!

SO YOU MISSPELL EVERY FIFTH WORD IN PROTEST?
OH, YOU NOTISED.
GB Trudeau

May 13, 2018

GRADUATING SENIORS...

NORMALLY ON THIS OCCASION, I TEND TO GENERALIZE ABOUT YOUR CLASS, INDEED ABOUT YOUR ENTIRE GENERATION.

AND IN FACT, THERE'S ENOUGH DATA TO FAIRLY CHARACTERIZE iGEN AS TOLERANT, ENTREPRENEURIAL, PRIVATE, ANXIOUS DIGITAL NATIVES!
WALDEN COLLEGE

BUT SINCE THOSE TRAITS ONLY DESCRIBE A MEAN, TODAY I'LL REFRAIN FROM LUMPING YOU TOGETHER AND ADDRESS YOU AS INDIVIDUALS!

SO! LET'S GET TO IT...
JENNA ABBOT, BE YOUR BEST SELF! DANIEL ABDULLA, LIFE IS A JOURNEY! THOMAS ABNER, OWN YOUR NARRATIVE...
GBTrudeau

... ALEX ABRAMS, TAKE AGENCY! ALFRED...
OH, MY GOD, LUMP US, LUMP US!
QUIET, ZACH ZELMAN!

May 27, 2018

THE FOLLOWING **PSA** IS BROUGHT TO YOU BY COMMON DECENCY.
HI, I'M NORM. OR NORMA. I MIGHT BE A REPUBLICAN OR A DEMOCRAT. AND I COULD BE WHITE OR BLACK, LATINO OR ASIAN. GAY, STRAIGHT, DOESN'T MATTER.
THE POINT IS, I'M YOUR NEXT PRESIDENT.

NOW, I'M FAR FROM PERFECT. LIKE ANYONE ELSE, I MAKE MISTAKES, GET FRUSTRATED, AND SOMETIMES LOSE MY TEMPER.
ALSO, I CAN BE FORGETFUL OR DISTRACTED, AND I COULD ALWAYS DO BETTER AS A PARENT.

BUT HERE'S WHAT ELSE I AM. I'M NICE. CIVIL. SERIOUS. THOUGHTFUL. IDEALISTIC. RESPONSIBLE. HONEST. COHERENT.
I'M EDUCATED, BUT I'M HUMBLE ABOUT WHAT I DON'T KNOW, SO I READ, LISTEN, PREPARE. I WORK HARD.

I VALUE KINDNESS. I'M EMPATHETIC, GRATEFUL. I RESPECT ALL PEOPLE, BUT ESPECIALLY THOSE WHO SERVE.
I'M PATRIOTIC, AND I CHERISH **ALL** OUR DEMOCRATIC INSTITUTIONS, PARTICULARLY OUR FREE PRESS.
I WORSHIP A LOVING GOD.

NOW, I KNOW WHAT YOU'RE THINKING – I'M TOO GOOD TO BE TRUE. BUT I'M NOT. I'M WHAT YOU'D EXPECT IN **ANY** PRESIDENT.
YOU'VE VOTED FOR ME IN THE PAST, AND IN TWO SHORT YEARS, YOU CAN VOTE FOR ME AGAIN!

SO DON'T LOSE HEART, AMERICA – NORM IS **ON THE WAY**!
THANK YOU.
DID I MENTION I WAS POLITE?
GBTrudeau

June 10, 2018

WHAT NOW?
SIR, THIS STORMY DANIELS THING WON'T GO AWAY...

WE'VE GOTTEN HUNDREDS OF CALLS FROM WOMEN WHO'VE NEVER HAD SEX WITH YOU – ALL DEMANDING $130,000 TO NOT SAY THEY HAVE!

THAT **DOES** IT! DANIELS IS GOING DOWN!
I'M NOT SURE YOU CAN TROLL YOUR WAY OUT OF THIS, SIR.

WHY **NOT**?
DANIELS IS A PORN STAR – BY DEFINITION, IMPERVIOUS TO SHAME.

WORSE, SHE'S **AMERICA'S** PORN STAR – FUNNY, LIKEABLE, CRED-IBLE – AND A NATURAL ON TV!
AND HER LAWYER'S AN EVEN **BIGGER** STAR!
GBTrudeau

THAT SCUM-BAG? HE CAN...
WAIT. SHOULD ANY OF THIS BE IN THE COMICS?
SURE. NEWS-PAPER READ-ERS ARE OLD.
TIME

June 17, 2018

August 30, 2015

OKAY, CANVASSERS, HERE'S THE **PITCH**!
WHEN YOU LOOK AT WHAT PASSES FOR POLICY IN TRUMPWORLD...

... CUTTING FOOD STAMPS AND MEDICAID, TRIPLING ASSISTED HOUSING RENTS, TEARING APART REFUGEE FAMILIES, ELIMINATING MEALS-ON-WHEELS AND HEATING FUEL ASSISTANCE, AND ON AND ON...

...THE CONTEMPT FOR THE VULNERABLE IS PALPABLE! IT'S THE MEANNESS, THE SHEER **CRUELTY** OF THESE PEOPLE THAT JUST FLOORS YOU!

SO ABOVE ALL, THAT'S WHAT THIS CAMPAIGN IS ABOUT, GANG – **NOT** BEING CRUEL!
EELER
Wheeler for Congr

GB Trudeau

WE'RE NOT **CRUEL**! WE'RE NOT **CRUEL**!
THAT'S IT?
GOOD PLACE TO START, NO?

June 24, 2018

SO LOOKS LIKE TRUMP COULD CATCH A BIG BREAK ON THE STEELE FILE.
HOW'S THAT?

DEEPFAKE VIDEO TECHNOLOGY – IT'S REALLY MATURED.

BAD ACTORS CAN NOW STITCH FACES ONTO THE BODIES OF, WELL, BAD ACTORS.

WHICH MEANS THAT IF PUTIN REALLY **DOES** HAVE VIDEO-TAPE OF TRUMP IN THAT MOSCOW HO-TEL ROOM...

... THE PRESIDENT NOW HAS DENIABILITY. HE CAN JUST DISMISS IT AS FAKE PORN.

GAME CHANGE!
WE KNEW YOU'D BE PLEASED, SIR.

July 1, 2018

SO I'M SENSING SOME REAL COMMON GROUND HERE, FOLKS...
VOTE
MAGA

WE AGREE EVERYONE'S ENTITLED TO ADEQUATE HEALTHCARE COVERAGE, TO CLEAN AIR AND WATER, TO A LIVING WAGE, TO PROTECTIONS FROM CONSUMER FRAUD...
MEL for Congress

... AND WE AGREE ON ECONOMIC INEQUALITY, THAT OUR POLITICAL SYSTEM UNFAIRLY FAVORS CORPORATIONS AND THE WEALTHY, WHO DON'T PAY THEIR FAIR SHARE!

WELL, THAT'S ALL TRUE, BUT WE ALSO SUPPORT THE PRESIDENT.
AND YOU DON'T. WHICH IS KIND OF A DEAL BREAKER FOR US...

SORRY TO WASTE YOUR TIME, MA'AM.
NOT AT ALL, SIR, IT WAS ONLY...
MAGA
VOTE
GBTrudeau

...AN HOUR AND A HALF?
YOU'RE NEW AT THIS, AREN'T YOU, HONEY?
MAGA
VOTE

July 8, 2018

B.D., DO YOU KNOW IF SAM IS SERIOUS ABOUT ANYONE NOW?

HAVEN'T A CLUE. BUT I'D BE THE LAST TO KNOW.
I DO HOPE SHE HOLDS OUT FOR A WHILE...

I ONCE READ THAT IN GUYS, THE BRAIN DEVELOPS LATE, ESPECIALLY THE PART THAT AFFECTS JUDGMENT AND IMPULSE CONTROL.
SU
FLO

YOU MEAN THE PREFRONTAL CORTEX?
THAT'S IT!

IN THE ARMY, WE HAD ANOTHER NAME FOR THE PREFRONTAL CORTEX...
WHAT'S THAT?
GBTrudeau

SERGEANTS.
GREAT IDEA! COULD YOU INTRODUCE HER TO ONE?

July 15, 2018

Roland B. Hedley Jr. @RealRBHJr
Hung w. John Bolton in college, always knew that one day he'd have a hand in deaths of thousands. Just a feeling you got when he walked into a room.

Roland B. Hedley Jr. @RealRBHJr
Being in White House "thoughts and prayers" widely misunderstood. Just means you're on their radar. No one's actually thinking or praying -- way too busy!

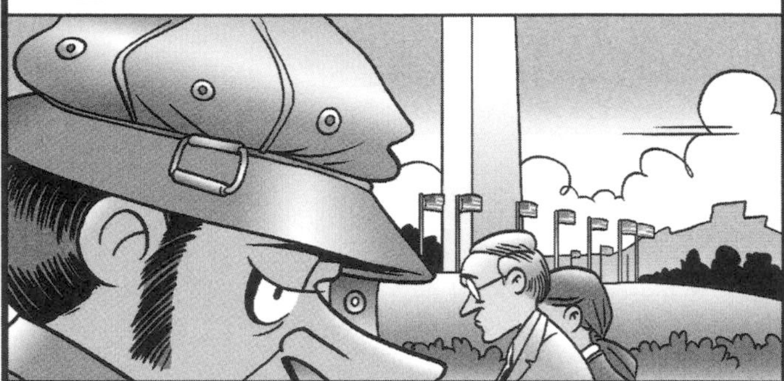

Roland B. Hedley Jr. @RealRBHJr
Banning Mercedes, BMWs, is tough, as dealers could smuggle them in from Alabama, S. Carolina, where they're made. Will need Stronger Borders!

Roland B. Hedley Jr. @RealRBHJr
NDA w. Playmate cost RNC official cool $1.6 M, while Prez got similar NDA for only $130K! Reputation as Best Negotiator Ever still intact!

Roland B. Hedley Jr. @RealRBHJr
WH continues to slash onerous spelling regs, announces new accepted spellings for collusion (collussion), missile (missle), Melania (Melanie).

Roland B. Hedley Jr. @RealRBHJr
Big #Win for "thousands" of Korean War parents who begged Prez to bring home remains of sons. Probably just in time, as average age is 115.

FOLLOW ROLAND ON TWITTER @ RealRBHJr

July 22, 2018

September 2, 2018

August 5, 2018

March 20, 2016

August 12, 2018

August 26, 2018

August 19, 2018

September 9, 2018

September 16, 2018

September 23, 2018

September 30, 2018

October 7, 2018

Roland B. Hedley Jr. @RealRBHJr
In sign that base now has more realistic expectations, rally cries of "Build that wall!" are giving way to new chants of "Renovate that fence!" Same fervor, though!

Roland B. Hedley Jr. @RealRBHJr
North Korea still building nukes. While POTUS says he had "a great chemistry" w. Kim, apparently they couldn't get the physics quite right.

Roland B. Hedley Jr. @RealRBHJr
In surprising development for such high-profile words, WH announces new accepted spellings for "collusion" (colusion), "counsel" (council) and "tariffs" (tarrifs).

Roland B. Hedley Jr. @RealRBHJr
Look for Fake Media to start addressing POTUS as "Mr. Unindicted Co-conspirator!" instead of "Mr. President!" So disrespectful!

Roland B. Hedley Jr. @RealRBHJr
As POTUS picks up tempo of false claims pre-mid-terms, intense WH debate on what historic 5,000th lie should be about. Has to be something very special!
GBTrudeau

Roland B. Hedley Jr. @RealRBHJr
Cut Trump some slack on family separations. He may never have heard his own kids crying when ripped out of arms of their regular nannies by weekend nannies.
FOLLOW ROLAND ON TWITTER @ RealRBHJr

October 14, 2018

October 21, 2018

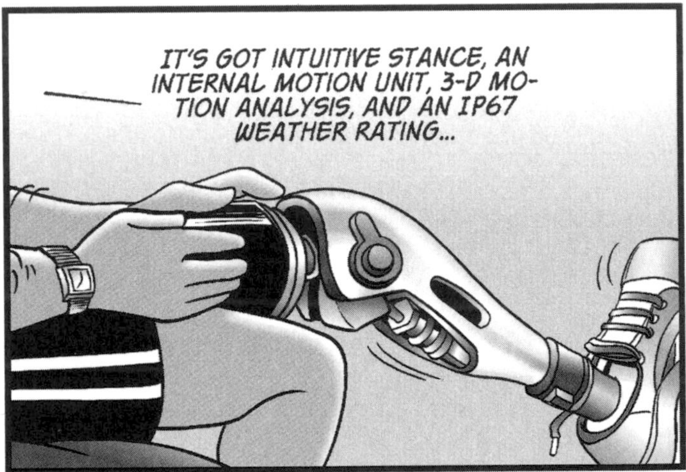

October 28, 2018

November 4, 2018

November 11, 2018

November 18, 2018

HEY, DREW, YOU WANT ICED... TEA? M-MAKING ...SOME!
LOVE SOME, LEO!
HUNH.

WHAT?
LEO DIDN'T EVEN LOOK UP WHEN YOU CAME IN.

UM... WHY WOULD HE?
HE USUALLY CHECKS YOU OUT. BUT HE'S A FATHER NOW...

... AND THE RESEARCH SHOWS THAT NEW FATHERS OFTEN EX-PERIENCE REDUCED SEX DRIVE!

THERE'S SOME EVIDENCE THAT IT'S TRIGGERED BY THE SMELL OF THEIR OWN CHILDREN...
GBTrudeau

WHAT IS?
L-L-LOOK GOOD TO-DAY, DREW!
THANKS, LEO.
I HATE JUNK SCIENCE.

June 21, 2015

November 25, 2018

WE'RE NOW IN THE PREFRONTAL CORTEX, HOME TO EXECUTIVE FUNCTION – PLANNING, JUDGMENT, AND SOCIAL CONTROL!
NOTHING HERE! ALL CLEAR!

PART 2

In Search of Trump's Brain

December 2, 2018

December 9, 2018

December 16, 2018

December 23, 2018

December 30, 2018

January 6, 2019

January 13, 2019

Roland B. Hedley Jr. @RealRBHJr
POTUS still steamed that Fake Media, by making big deal of 41's "selflessness," "courage," "competence," etc., was trafficking in blatant subtext. So insulting!

Roland B. Hedley Jr. @RealRBHJr
Ivanka/Clinton comparisons are a disgrace. Crooked stored email on secret basement server, while First D used public server anyone could hack! #Transparency

Roland B. Hedley Jr. @RealRBHJr
Overheard my kids planning to use fake IDs to buy cereal, per POTUS. When busted, they claimed they were joking, not who they were as teenagers.

Roland B. Hedley Jr. @RealRBHJr
Source: Frustrated by pace of Caravan, slowed by strollers, walkers, the White House tried to bus criminal invaders to US border in time for mid-terms.

6X
WS

Roland B. Hedley Jr. @RealRBHJr
As his grandparents, mother, two wives, in-laws are all immigrants, POTUS shows best moral courage to vilify immigrants. Personally painful, but #CountryFirst!

Roland B. Hedley Jr. @RealRBHJr
Breaking: In addition to unsecure phone, POTUS also uses two insecure phones to call friends to see how he's doing. Smart!

FOLLOW ROLAND
ON TWITTER
@ RealRBHJr

January 20, 2019

February 3, 2019

February 10, 2019

February 17, 2019

February 24, 2019

November 10, 2019

March 10, 2019

March 17, 2019

March 24, 2019

Donald J. Trump @realDonaldTrump
The many, many "people" who were affected by my shutdown are still in my Thoughts and Prayers, believe me.

March 31, 2019

SO SHE WANTS TO RENT A ROOM FROM US?
UM... NO. SHE CAN'T AFFORD TO.

WHY NOT?
ANGELA'S HOMELESS. SHE'S LIV-ING IN HER CAR.

A WALDEN STUDENT IS **HOMELESS**?
HER SCHOLARSHIP DOESN'T COVER ROOM AND BOARD. AND SHE'S NOT THE ONLY ONE.

THAT'S AWFUL!
SO I JUST THOUGHT SINCE WE HAVE SO MANY EMPTY BED-ROOMS...

WELL, WALDEN **HAS** BEEN A COMMUNE AND A REFUGEE SANCTUARY. I SEE NO REASON WHY IT COULDN'T BECOME A HOMELESS SHELTER!!
GBTrudeau

MY DEAD BODY?
HOW MANY SHOULD WE EXPECT?
NOT SURE. YOU WORK ON DAD, I'LL BRING HER STUFF IN.

April 7, 2019

Roland B. Hedley Jr. @RealRBHJr
Christie would be inspired choice for Chief of Staff. Already soiled by scandal, humiliated by Trump, no future, so could skip those steps!

Roland B. Hedley Jr. @RealRBHJr
If $5.6B Border Wall becomes reality, Sinaloa Cartel reportedly prepared to counter by investing $56,000 in new tunnel infrastructure.

Roland B. Hedley Jr. @RealRBHJr
Source: Trump may propose protecting border not with Wall but with Red Line. Unlike Obama, would act strongly against anyone crossing it.

Roland B. Hedley Jr. @RealRBHJr
Trump calls Tim Cook "Tim Apple" to "save time." We all do this. If I had a nickel for every time I've said "Mark Facebook," I'd be rich as Donald Russia.

Roland B. Hedley Jr. @RealRBHJr
Betting POTUS's idea of holding parade in DC on July 4th will catch on around nation. Adding fireworks nice touch! Something very special!

Roland B. Hedley Jr. @RealRBHJr
To avoid being technically "obese," Trump to use Exec Order to increase height to 6'5". WH doc now says he has "heart, lungs of a dragon."

FOLLOW ROLAND
ON TWITTER
@ RealRBHJr

April 14, 2019

April 21, 2019

April 28, 2019

HI, KIDS! YES, IT'S ME, **JUULY**, MR. E-CIG HIMSELF!

BY NOW, YOU KNOW THAT VAPING HAS CAPTURED THE IMAGINATION OF MILLIONS OF YOUNGSTERS JUST LIKE **YOURSELF**!

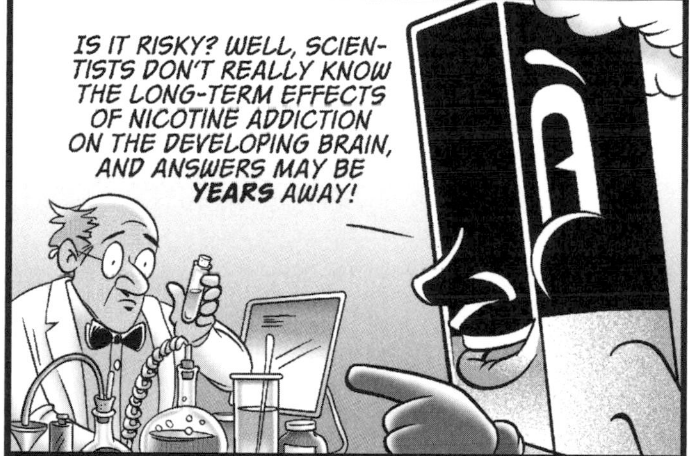
IS IT RISKY? WELL, SCIENTISTS DON'T REALLY KNOW THE LONG-TERM EFFECTS OF NICOTINE ADDICTION ON THE DEVELOPING BRAIN, AND ANSWERS MAY BE **YEARS** AWAY!

?
SO WHILE WE'RE WAITING, WHY MISS OUT ON THE CRAZE THAT **EVERYONE** IS...
CUT!

WHAT? WHAT DID I FORGET?
ME, DUDE! YOU'RE A GATEWAY FOR **ME**! **SELL** IT!
CUT!
MR. B

WHO'S THIS?
BEAT IT, MIKE! THIS IS **MY** NIGHTMARE!
OH...
WHEW!

May 5, 2019

WONDER HOW ROLAND'S INTERVIEW WENT THIS MORNING...

IT DIDN'T HAPPEN. GOT RESCHEDULED.

HE'S IN THE OVAL OFFICE DOING IT RIGHT NOW.

WHY'D IT GET BUMPED?
APPARENTLY, POTUS IS HAVING ONE OF HIS 25TH AMEND-MENT DAYS. THEY HAD TO FIND A TRANSLATOR.
GBTrudeau

TRANSLATOR?

MY ORANGES ARE IN GERMANY, ROLAND FOX!
HE SAYS HIS GRANDFATHER WAS BORN IN GERMANY.
TELL HIM THAT'S AMAZING!

May 12, 2019

ALRIGHT, LISTEN UP, EVERYONE!
UH-OH...

I WASN'T ACTUALLY CON-SULTED ABOUT TURNING THIS PLACE INTO A SHEL-TER FOR HOMELESS STUDENTS...

... SO LET'S GET A FEW THINGS STRAIGHT! FIRST, THIS IS **NOT** A COLLEGE CAMPUS! THERE ARE **NO** SAFE SPACES IN THIS HOUSE. I'LL SAY WHATEVER I DAMN WELL PLEASE!

SO IF I TRIGGER YOU WITH SOME DUMB MICRO-AGGRESSION, COMPLAIN TO SOMEONE WHO CARES! ALSO NO DRUGS, NO RAP MUSIC AND NO SERVICE PETS!

LASTLY, I HATE LAWSUITS, SO KEEP YOUR HANDS TO YOUR-SELVES! NO SHOULDER RUBS, BUTT CUPPING OR HAIR SMELLING! ANY QUESTIONS?

YES, WHO SMELLS HAIR? IS THAT A THING?
DAD, YOU...
ANGELA! WHERE'RE YOU GOING?
BACK TO MY CAR. I CAN'T LIVE LIKE THIS.
GBTrudeau

May 19, 2019

I KNOW SOME PEOPLE ARE SAYING I'M TOO **OLD** TO BE PRESI- DENT...
... UNLIKE MAYOR PETE!

HA! SEE THAT? **PETE BUTTIGIEG** JUST "MADE" THE STRIP...
... A PRESTIGIOUS PLACEMENT SEEN ACROSS THE NATION!
ON AIR

HOW'D IT HAPPEN? WELL, IT WAS NO ACCIDENT! HIS PEOPLE BOOKED TODAY'S MENTION **MONTHS** AGO! AND NOW **YOU** CAN, TOO!

IF YOU'RE RUNNING FOR PRESIDENT - AND WHO **ISN'T** THESE DAYS? - WE'RE OFFERING COM- PLIMENTARY EXPOSURE TO **ALL** QUALIFIED CANDI- DATES AS A PUBLIC SERVICE!

SURE, YOU MIGHT BE MERCILESSLY MOCKED - IT **IS** A COMIC STRIP...
... BUT THAT'S ALL PART OF THE FUN!
SO BE LIKE PETE AND BOOK YOUR FREE SHOUT- OUT **TODAY**!
GBTrudeau

OH, AND IF YOU ACT NOW, WE'LL ALSO NAME-CHECK YOUR SPOUSE! OR NOT!
YOUR CALL.
CHASTEN!

May 26, 2019

LASTLY, ON THIS MOST GLORIOUS OF DAYS, DO **NOT** FORGET TO THANK YOUR PARENTS!
WALDEN UNIVERSITY

IT'S ONLY THROUGH THEIR SACRIFICES THAT YOU NOW GO FORTH INTO THE WORLD AS PROUD WALDEN GRADUATES!

EVEN THOSE PARENTS WHO CHEATED TO GAIN YOUR ADMISSION HERE DESERVE GRATITUDE...

... GRATITUDE FOR THEIR WILLINGNESS TO DO **ANYTHING** TO MAKE SURE YOU SUCCEED IN LIFE!

NEVER MIND THAT THEY RISKED JAIL FOR NOTH-ING, AS WALDEN ACTUALLY ADMITS **ANYONE** WHO CAN PAY THEIR OWN WAY.
GBTrudeau

D'OH!
SHHH!
I TOLD YOU!

June 2, 2019

... EVERYONE'S
STILL MARVELING
OVER THE 104 LIES
YOU PACKED INTO
YOUR TWO-HOUR
CPAC SPEECH!

PART 3

Lie 10,000

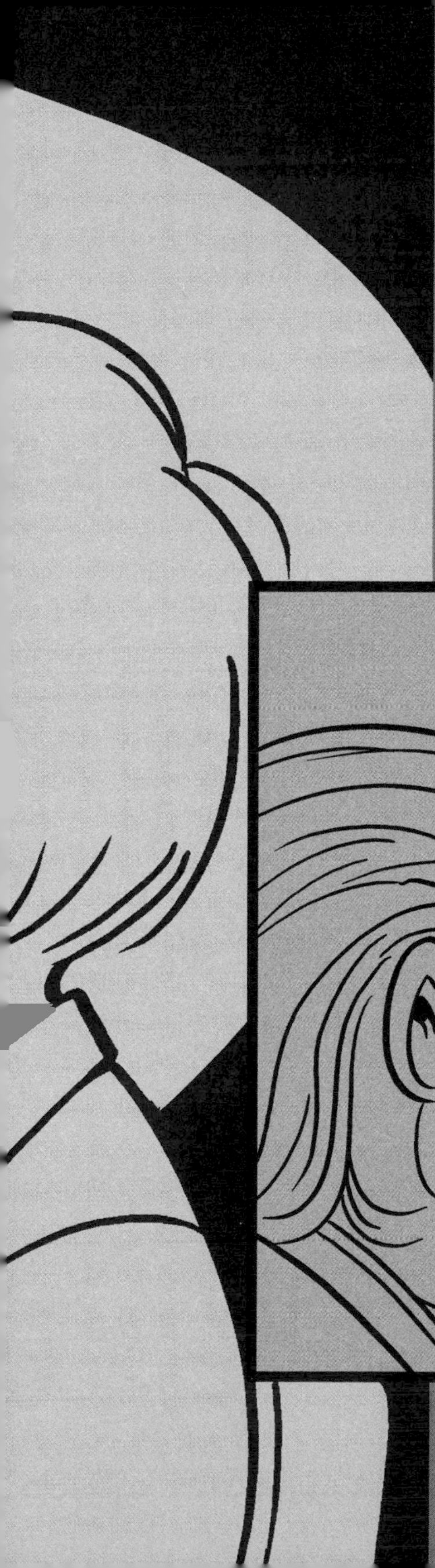

SO?

SO MANY PEOPLE WONDER HOW YOU **DO** IT!

♫!
UNCLE Z? HOW COME THE NEWS NEVER SEEMS TO GET YOU DOWN?

WELL, NEPHEW, I DON'T LET IT. I THINK ABOUT WHAT THE GRUNTS IN VIETNAM USED TO SAY WHEN STUFF GOT UGLY...
"IT DON'T MEAN NOTHIN'!"

OH... IS THAT LIKE "IT IS WHAT IT IS"?
EXACTLY!

LIFE BECOMES MORE BEARABLE IF YOU JUST TAKE THINGS AS THEY COME...

ONCE YOU ACCEPT THAT HORRI-BLE IS THE NEW NORMAL, YOU CAN JUST ROLL WITH IT!
GBTrudeau

FOR INSTANCE, I ACTUALLY ENJOYED LAST WEEK'S FOURTH OF TRUMP.
HEY, ME TOO! BEST HOLIDAY EVER!

July 7, 2019

SO MUCH FOR STROKING. HOW ARE WE FIXED FOR GRIEVANCE TODAY?
I'LL BE TRIGGERING THE PRESIDENT ON IMMIGRATION. SEAN'S HANDLING MUELLER.
FOX NEWS

ANYTHING WE CAN GIN UP ON McCAIN?
WE'VE GOT SOME TAPE OF THE NUT-TY DAUGHTER WE COULD DOCTOR.

NO, WE MAY WANT TO ROLL OUT SOME DEEPFAKE VIDEOS OF BIDEN SOON. LET'S KEEP OUR POWDER DRY.

OKAY, ANY CONSPIRACIES WE WANT POTUS TO HIT TODAY?
HOW ABOUT THE FBI IS "TREASON-OUS"?

DO WE KNOW IF HE CAN SPELL IT?
NO, BUT HE LOVES SAY-ING IT!
OKAY, LET'S GIVE IT TO "FOX AND FRIENDS."

SO HOW TREASON-OUS IS THE FBI?
"EVERYBODY IS SAYING THE FBI IS TREESONOUS!"
TOTALLY!
OUT OF CONTROL!
GBTrudeau

July 14, 2019

February 4, 2018

WHAT ARE YOU DOING, KID?
UH... I'M HUN-GRY, COACH...

I DON'T RECALL OFFER-ING YOU GUYS A MEAL PLAN WITH YOUR FREE RENT!
IT'S AN EMERGENCY. I SUFFER FROM FOOD INSECURITY.

YOU MAY NOT BE AWARE OF THE HIGH PERCENTAGE OF STUDENTS WHO GO HUNGRY AT SOME TIME!

KID, IN MY EXPERIENCE, **100%** OF COLLEGE STU-DENTS ARE HUNGRY **ALL** THE TIME!

AND JUST BECAUSE YOU'RE FEELING "INSECURE" DOESN'T MEAN YOU'RE ENTITLED TO PILFER FOOD WITHOUT **ASKING**!
OKAY, OKAY.
GBTrudeau

SIR? WOULD YOU HAVE ANY PROTEIN YOU'RE NOT USING?
SEE? MANNERS!
GIMME THOSE EGGS!

June 16, 2019

HEY, ZIP, I NEED YOU TO SWEEP OUT THE DRYING SHED, OKAY?
AGAIN?
Z+Z BUD

SEE, THIS IS WHY WE NEED A HIRED HAND– I'M A **FOUNDER** OF Z+Z BUD, NOT THE BARN BOY!

IF WE HAD A HIRED HAND, I COULD FOCUS ON THE BUSINESS PLAN! WE COULD SCALE UP AND FINALLY **GROW** THE COMPANY!

IN FACT, WE COULD DISRUPT THE WHOLE INDUSTRY, ROCK A MASSIVE IPO, AND RETIRE AS BOY BILLIONAIRES!

YOU'RE NOT GO-ING TO SWEEP OUT THE SHED, ARE YOU?
DON'T YOU SEE? WE'RE **THAT** CLOSE! WE COULD BE FREAKIN' **UNICORNS!**

OKAY, SO WHICH ONE OF US IS HIGH?
I THINK IT'S MY TURN.
I COULD BE WRONG. WHY?
GBTrudeau

June 23, 2019

GUESS WHO, EVIL-DOERS!
GASP! IT'S SORKH RAZIL, A.K.A. THE RED RASP-BERRY!

THAT'S RASCAL! RED RASCAL!
IT'S THE RED RASCAL! BUT WHY IS HE HERE IN TEHRAN?

WELL, IF YOU MUST KNOW, HE'S IN TOWN TO AFFECT RE-GIME CHANGE, TO TAKE OUT THE TYRANT!

SO WHERE IS HE? WHERE'S THE SU-PREME LEADER?
KHAMENEI? HE'S COWER-ING UNDER THE TABLE!

MERCY, RED RAS-CAL!
SORRY, LOSER! JOHN BOLTON SENDS HIS RE-GARDS!

WHO'S JOHN BOLTON?
NO IDEA. HE SIGNED THE WORK ORDER.
GBTrudeau

June 30, 2019

SO, POP – WHO'S GONNA TAKE IT NEXT YEAR?
WHO DO YOU THINK?

THE SOUTHERN DISTRICT HAS INDIVIDUAL ONE IN THEIR CROSS-HAIRS, BUT AS LONG AS HE STAYS PRESIDENT, HE'S UNTOUCHABLE!

SO IN A TIGHT RACE, WHO DO YOU LIKE – SOME DOOFUS DEMOCRAT WITH "SOLUTIONS FOR AMERICA"...

... OR A DESPERATE, FERAL POTUS FIGHTING TOOTH AND NAIL TO STAY OUT OF PRISON?

WELL...
WHAT DID I TEACH YOU AS A KID?
GB Trudeau

"ALWAYS BET ON THE CORNERED RAT."
AND YOU NEVER LOST A **DIME**, RIGHT? RIGHT?

July 21, 2019

Roland B. Hedley Jr. @RealRBHJr
Still torn re: college cheating scandal. Never like to see attractive actresses taken into custody, but also hate to see hedge fund managers free on bail.

Roland B. Hedley Jr. @RealRBHJr
On 180th golf outing, POTUS playful as he kicked errant ball back on fairway. "I'm happier than all previous presidents combined!" he screamed at me.

Roland B. Hedley Jr. @RealRBHJr
I'm old enough to remember when it was hilarious to say you were old enough to remember something that happened recently.

Roland B. Hedley Jr. @RealRBHJr
Seven indicted Trump aides must be kicking selves. If POTUS is totally innocent, why did they all perjure themselves? These guys too dumb NOT to be in jail!

Roland B. Hedley Jr. @RealRBHJr
Forgotten Notre Dame fire? Fox Foreign News desk hasn't, still sending #ThoughtsNPrayers to people of Rome. We're all European Unionists now. #Sad

Roland B. Hedley Jr. @RealRBHJr
At the White House 10K Alternative Facts Afterparty, learned what POTUS's 10,000th lie was. Referring to his 9,999th lie, Trump said, "It's only 9,998!" LOL

July 28, 2019

August 4, 2019

August 11, 2019

August 18, 2019

August 25, 2019

September 1, 2019

October 20, 2019

THE FUTURE TWEETS OF DONALD J. TRUMP
Donald J. Trump @realDonaldTrump
Have strongly ordered Justice Dept and My Generals to nullifie terrible "election," a complete & total Fraud in which 13 million immigrants, rapists & Russians "voted"!

Donald J. Trump @realDonaldTrump
Second Disgusting, Phony Trial has begun with highly-biased juree that has many, so many Blacks and "women" on it like no one would believe possible! Total Which Hunt!

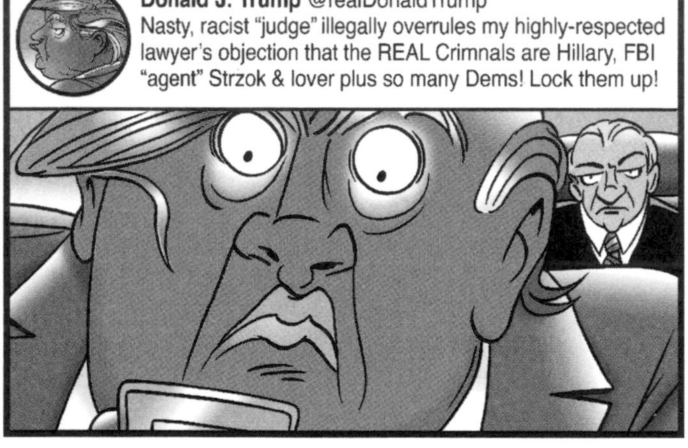
Donald J. Trump @realDonaldTrump
Nasty, racist "judge" illegally overrules my highly-respected lawyer's objection that the REAL Crimnals are Hillary, FBI "agent" Strzok & lover plus so many Dems! Lock them up!

Donald J. Trump @realDonaldTrump
Losing 1st & 2nd Amendment Rites of our great Constitution. Also, keys, wallet, phone, but Base won't stand for there favorite President treeted so poorly! My Judges will overturn!

Donald J. Trump @realDonaldTrump
Using phone traded me by J.T. Ridley, new owner of Trump Winerys. He and fellow Corrections Officers are something very special. Know he'll make Wine like no one ever has!
GBTrudeau

Donald J. Trump @realDonaldTrump
Was misinformed by very stupid advisers about MS-13. "Gang" actually a beautiful thing, with some Very Fine members like "El Gato," "Muerto," & "Chucky." The Best!!

September 15, 2019

September 22, 2019

September 29, 2019

SO! HOW'S CAMP GO-ING, GUYS?
GREAT!
YEAH, THEY SEEM TO LOVE IT.

H-H-HOW... ABOUT YOU, MA? EVERYTHING GOOD?

YEAH, FEWER ILLEGALS IN THE TRAILER PARK NOW. EVER SINCE TRUMP.
UH-OH...

I JUST LOVE, LOVE, LOVE THE PRESIDENT! SAY WHAT YOU WILL ABOUT...
EXCUSE ME, GRAMMY.

GBTrudeau

YOU TRAINED THEM TO LEAVE THE ROOM?
NO, NO, THEY DO IT ON THEIR OWN!
IT... PROGRES-SIVE CAMP.

July 29, 2018

HI, KIDS! LIES, SPIN AND CONSPIRACY THEORY MAY RULE AT THE WHITE HOUSE, BUT **REAL** LIFE IS A BOX OF **FACTS**!
HERE'S A CURATED COLLECTION OF OUR FAVES!* ENJOY!
37
28
80
210
0
0
1,397
40
34
24
BEST IF USED BEFORE: NOV. 3 2020
CERTIFIED 100% TRUE by Mr Google
BIG BO
*ALL FAC

October 6, 2019

October 13, 2019

September 8, 2019

October 27, 2019

November 3, 2019

November 17, 2019

CAN YOU SAY, "MAMA," ROSIE? "MAMA"?
NO WORDS YET?

NOT ACTUAL WORDS. LOTS OF SYLLABLES, THOUGH.

I FEEL LIKE A REAL WORD WILL POP OUT ANY DAY...

I JUST HOPE IT'S NOT "WALL."
WHAT WERE HER BROTHERS' FIRST WORDS?

HMM... LET'S SEE. I THINK DANNY'S FIRST WORDS WERE "MORE CAKE." ELI'S WAS "MOON."
GB Trudeau

NEVERTHE-LESS, SHE PERSISTED!
ROSIE!
WOW. GREAT START!

March 3, 2019

THE CONTINUING TWEETS OF ROLAND B. HEDLEY.
Roland B. Hedley Jr. @RealRBHJr
Source: With Ukraine and China off table, POTUS tells aides he's now open to accepting Dirt from "sh- - - - - - countries," provided Dirt is in English.
Roland B. Hedley Jr. @RealRBHJr
Contrast Alert: Obama initiated 13,000 infrastructure projects, improving 42,000 miles road, 2,700 bridges, but never held a SINGLE Infrastructure Week. #Sad!
Roland B. Hedley Jr. @RealRBHJr
In Year 1, Obama built 130 miles new border fencing. POTUS has built zero, but completed more miles of Scheduled Fence Maintenance than anyone!
Roland B. Hedley Jr. @RealRBHJr
When POTUS learned U.S. already has 1,248 mile moat (Rio Grande), wanted to take credit for digging it. Sadly, moat already appeared in too many movies.
Roland B. Hedley Jr. @RealRBHJr
26 more attention-seekers accusing Trump of sexual misconduct, for total of 50. Still shy of Bill Cosby's record of 60, but Easy for POTUS to overtake!
Roland B. Hedley Jr. @RealRBHJr
POTUS occasionally tone-deaf, which is when Statute of Limitations comes in handy. "Not my type" not usually well-received by juries in rape trials.
Roland B. Hedley Jr. @RealRBHJr
WH to set up Condolence Center on Mall to collect, bundle Prayers for next mass shooting. Thoughts to be separated out, stored in local GOP think tanks.
Roland B. Hedley Jr. @RealRBHJr
Report: President vetoed background checks when he realized it's not person who pulls trigger, it's finger. Already have finger background checks (fingerprints).
Roland B. Hedley Jr. @RealRBHJr
Israel renames Golan Heights settlement "Trump Heights." With no funding, planning, location, Bibi pays fitting tribute to Actual Trump Projects!
GBTrudeau
FOLLOW ROLAND TWEETS @ Real RBHJr

November 24, 2019

December 1, 2019

SO IN A TIGHT RACE, WHO DO YOU LIKE – SOME DOOFUS DEM-OCRAT WITH "SOLUTIONS FOR AMERICA"...

PART 4

Cornering the Rat

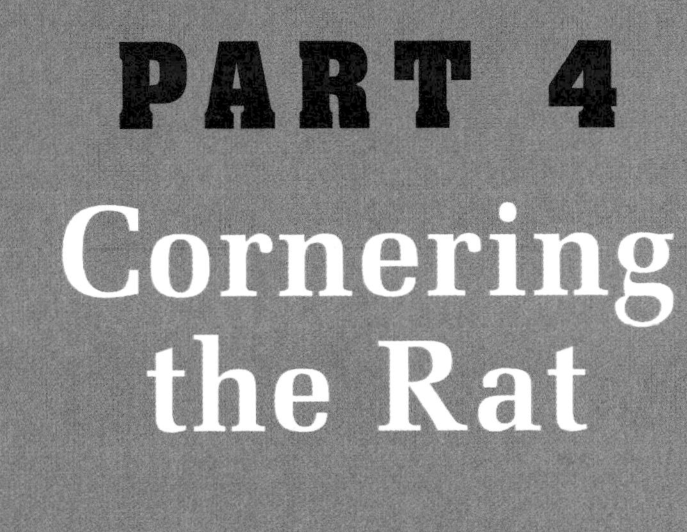

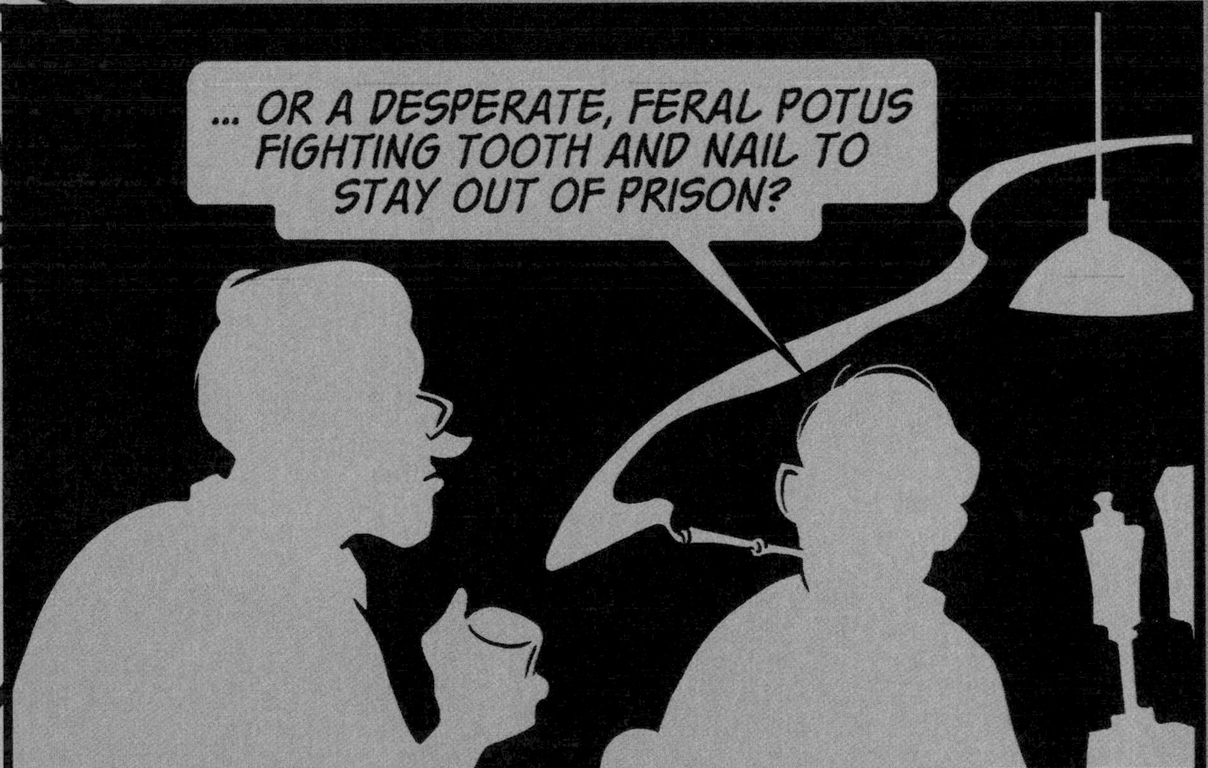

December 8, 2019

December 22, 2019

December 29, 2019

January 27, 2019

January 5, 2020

January 12, 2020

January 19, 2020

January 26, 2020

February 2, 2020

February 9, 2020

February 16, 2020

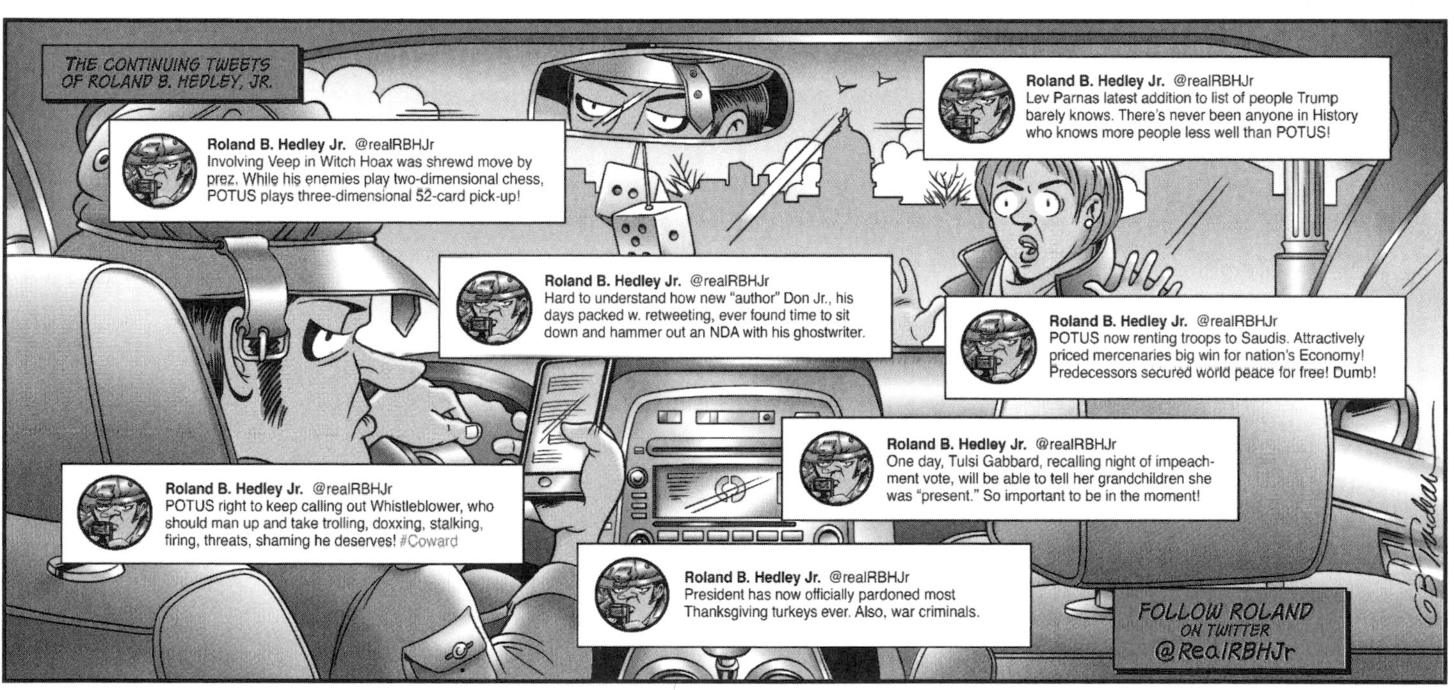

February 23, 2020

ANYWAY, WE'RE HOPING EDDIE GALLAGHER AND MY OTHER PARDONED WAR CRIMINALS...

... WILL COME TO MAGA RALLIES TO BE SALUTED AS THE **HEROES** THEY ARE, MAY-BE THE BIGGEST **EVER**!

BUT, SIR, IF WAR CRIMINALS ARE NOW HEROES...
MY

WHAT DOES THAT MAKE THE MILLIONS OF MILI-TARY PERSONNEL...

... WHO HONORABLY SERVED THE NATION **WITHOUT** COMMITTING ATROCITIES?

WUSSES! THEY WEREN'T ALL IN!
I'M...CON-FUSED.
WELL, YOU **DO** HAVE A BRAIN INJURY.
GB Trudeau

March 1, 2020

LETTERS! YOU WRITE 'EM – WE READ 'EM!
SO LET'S GET RIGHT TO IT!
AIL

"DEAR MIKE, YOU GUYS SHOULD DO SOME HUMOROUS BIT ON ALL THE FORMERLY RESPECTED PEOPLE WHO SOILED THEIR REPUTATIONS BY KISSING UP TO TRUMP. REGARDS, BETSY F."
U.S. MA

NOT A BAD IDEA, MIKE. IF ONLY WE HAD THE ROOM.
TRUE THAT. IT'S QUITE A LIST...

REX TILLERSON, LINDSEY GRAHAM, WILLIAM BARR, JEFF SESSIONS, KIRSTJEN NIELSEN, REINCE PRIEBUS AND ON AND ON! NONE WILL **EVER** RECOVER THEIR GOOD NAMES!

DON'T FORGET ALAN DERSHOWITZ! ONCE A SERIOUS LEGAL SCHOLAR, NOW A **TOTAL** JOKE!
USMAIL

I'M **NOT** A JOKE!
DUDE. YOU'RE IN A COMIC STRIP.
YEAH, THAT'S NEVER GOOD.
GBTrudeau

March 8, 2020

March 15, 2020

March 22, 2020

March 29, 2020

JOEY FROM NEWARK, WHAT'S UP, MAN?
YES, MARK, I'M WORRIED THAT BILL BARR HAS TRASHED HIS REPUTATION! SHOULD I BE?

NOT AT ALL, JOEY! WHAT YOU MAY NOT KNOW ABOUT OUR ATTORNEY GENERAL...

... IS THAT THE **LAST** TIME HE WAS AG, HE URGED BUSH TO PARDON SIX OF THE IRAN-CONTRA CONSPIRATORS...

... INCLUDING CASPAR WEINBERGER, WHO MIGHT HAVE IMPLICATED BUSH **HIMSELF** IN HIS PENDING TRIAL!

SO YOU SEE, JOEY, BARR WAS ALREADY AN OLD HAND AT COVERING UP PRESIDENTIAL CRIMES...
HE HAD NO REPUTATION FOR INTEGRITY **LEFT** TO TRASH!
WHAT A RELIEF! THANKS, MARK!
GBTrudeau

NO CHARGE, JOEY!
LEO FROM HOUSTON, YOU'RE **ON**!
YEAH, MARK, I'M WORRIED ABOUT JOHN BOLTON...

April 5, 2020

April 12, 2020

April 26, 2020

LOOK AT WHO STILL HAS ALL HIS HAIR!
HA!
WHO SAYS IT'S HIS?
HA! HA!
OKAY, SETTLE DOWN, GUYS. THANKS FOR ZOOMING IN.

AS CLASS REUNION CHAIR, I'D LIKE TO PROPOSE A TOAST...
EVERYONE GOT A DRINK?

TO THE MOST BADASS WALDEN CLASS **EVER**!

TO THE MOST BADASS WALDEN CLASS **EVER**!

NICE.

OKAY, GUYS, SEE YOU IN FIVE YEARS.
IF WE'RE LUCKY.
TAKE CARE.
WIPE YOUR KEYBOARDS, PEOPLE!
GBTrudeau

May 3, 2020

SO I CALL THE WHITE HOUSE, OKAY? TRUMP SAYS HE'S GOT MY BACK AND THAT EASTER IS **ON**!

SO I'M RARIN' TO GO, RIGHT? I'M DYEING UNITS LIKE A MAD-MAN, WORKING OUT MY ROUTES...

HE'D ALREADY GOTTEN MY HOPES UP BY SAY-ING THE VIRUS WOULD DISAPPEAR "LIKE A MIRACLE"!

WELL, EASTER'S ALL **ABOUT** MIRA-CLES, RIGHT? WITHOUT MAGICAL THINKING, YOU GOT NO RESUR-RECTION AND YOU GOT NO **ME**!

GOOD POINT.
SO ANYWAY, I HIT THE TRAIL AND GUESS WHAT? PEOPLE WON'T EVEN COME TO THE **DOOR**! I HAD TO EAT MY **ENTIRE** INVENTORY!

ROUGH. DID YOU GET A BAILOUT?
YEAH, RIGHT. WHAT DO I LOOK LIKE, AN AIRLINE?
GBTrudeau

May 10, 2020

WHAT WE'RE DOING IS, LIKE, **INCREDIBLE**! LIKE ONE OF THE GREAT JOBS EVER! LIKE... LIKE...
UH-OH.
WHAT?

BY THE WAY, WE LOVE OUR VETS! THAT I CAN STRONG-LY TELL YOU!
HIS WORKING VOCABULARY JUST DIPPED BELOW 100 WORDS. HE'S STRUGGLING!

SO WHAT WE'RE DOING IS VERY SPECIAL LIKE NOBODY BELIEVED POSSIBLE!
GO GET HIS BEST WORDS LIST!
ON IT!

PEOPLE ARE SAYING THEY CAN'T BELIEVE HOW UNBELIEVABLE IT IS!
HOLD ON, SIR! HELP IS ON THE WAY!
GOT IT!

SO WE'LL HAVE TO SEE. WE'LL BE LOOKING AT IT STRONGLY, BECAUSE IT'S SO INCREDIBLE!
HERE YOU GO, SIR.

"BACK-UP!" WE'RE LIKE "BACK-UP"!
A LOT OF PEOPLE DON'T KNOW THAT!
WHEW!
GBTrudeau

May 17, 2020

THE CONTINUING TWEETS OF ROLAND B. HEDLEY, JR.
Roland B. Hedley Jr. @RealRBHJr White House announces final division of responsibilities in Coronavirus Task Force. Deb Birx: Thoughts. Mike Pence: Prayers.
Roland B. Hedley Jr. @RealRBHJr Trump is wartime prez just like FDR. In WWII, states strongly sent troops to Europe, Pacific, while Federal government, FDR, were back-up.
Roland B. Hedley Jr. @RealRBHJr All governors late in locking down their states are Republican. Obviously coincidental, but need to act before "stupid" permanently baked into brand.
Roland B. Hedley Jr. @RealRBHJr POTUS go-to word at pressers is "incredible." "Incredible" means impossible to believe, so Trump responsibly signaling public not to try.
Roland B. Hedley Jr. @RealRBHJr Trump just introduced new term of art for coronavirus positive: "not perfect." Hundreds of thousands of Americans are now not perfect.
Roland B. Hedley Jr. @RealRBHJr POTUS uses special, marveling tone when he learns new terms like "pandemic" or "hot spots." That's the little boy in him – such fun to watch!
Roland B. Hedley Jr. @RealRBHJr Trump ripped for inaction, but the one time he acts prophylactically – telling doctors not to steal supplies – people go nuts! POTUS can't win!
FOLLOW ROLAND ON TWITTER @RealRBHJr
GBTrudeau

May 24, 2020

achomlishments (accomplishments) Alcaida (Al Qaeda) alowe (allowed) Amendmen (Amendment) apologizes (apologies) are (our) attaker (attacker) Barrack (Barack) Bengahzi (Banghazi Bidan (Biden) Boarder Security (border) capital (capito chanded (changed) cheif (chief) chocked (choked) chocker (choke covfefe (coverage) Columbia (Colombia) colusion (collusio Marine Core (Corps) councel (counsel) council (counsel) dieing (dying) discgrace (disgrace) discribing (describing) W.E.B. DeBois (DuBois) do (due) dummer (dumber) eminent (imminent) Esperanto (Esper) Generel (General) hamberder (hamburgers) hear by (hereby) hearby (hereby) heel (heal) highjacked (hijacked) honer (honor) honerd (honored) honered (honored) Hose Republicans (House) inocent (innocent) its (it's) it's (its) Kim Jung Un (Kim Jong Un) Bobby Nigh (Knight) leightweight (lightweight) liable (libel) loose (lose) tex massages (messages) Melanie (Melania) missle (missile) moo (moat) Deven Nunez (Devin Nunes) outrages (outrageous) payed (paid) peach (peace) principal (principle) prople (people) pour (pore) privet (private) reaspected (respected) roll (role) Rupublicans (Republicans) San Bernadino (San Bernardino) Secretary of Educa uon (Education) seperation (separation) Sepulcher (Sepulchre shoild (should) shoker (shocker) Smocking Gun (smoking Somolia (Somalia) tapp (tap) tarrifs (tariffs) Teresa May (Theresa) to (too) unpresidented (unprecedented) waist (waste) waite (wait) wether (whether) wonerful (wonderful Chinese President Xi Xinping (Jinping) Zellinsky (Zelensky